ne

Somewhere a blind child

Ion Cristofor discovers the world as he discovers the poem, which he creates obsessively in an imaginary laboratory. Sensuality and spirituality coexist in a recurring natural world, giving rise to a curious mix of cynicism and purity. This serves the basis of his poetry's characteristic compassion which sets him apart from fellow members of the '80s Generation': Romania's leading literary current of confessional poets who endured the harshest part of the communist regime and witnessed and wrote about the events preceding and following the 1989 Revolution.

Cristofor's poems leave the door open to possibilities: there is always more beneath the surface. A self-possessed seeker who builds upon his most authentic self with unwavering direction, he is a poet to welcome into the English language with open arms.

Ion Cristofor (b.1952) is a poet, literary critic, and translator with a doctorate in Romanian literature. He is former editor of *Echinox* journal and a member of the leading literary circle of the same name. He has published over twenty books of poetry and essays, some of which have been translated into Italian, German, French, and Catalan. In addition to his many awards in his native Romania, Cristofor has received the University of Freiburg's Publication Prize and an honorary diploma of membership from the Romanian-Israeli Cultural Centre in Haifa, Israel. Authors he has translated into Romanian include Tahashi Arima, Alain Petre, Alain Jadot, Paul Emond, Philippe Jones, and Liliane Wouters. He has translated, coordinated, and edited anthologies of poetry from Japan and Tunisia.

Andreea Iulia Scridon (b.1997) is a poet and translator. She studied Comparative Literature at King's College London and Creative Writing at the University of Oxford. Her translation of a series of short stories by Ion D. Sîrbu, a representative of subversive writing under the communist regime, is published in 2021 with ABPress, and her co-translations with Adam J. Sorkin of the Romanian poet Traian T. Coșovei are published with Broken Sleep Books (2021). She has a poetry pamphlet forthcoming with Broken Sleep Books and a poetry book forthcoming with MadHat Press in 2022.

Reviews of Ion Cristofor's poetry

Ion Cristofor's poetry is grave and troubled, but never sombre ... The naturalness of his poetry invites reflection and redemption, a recalibration of existential fact. Irina Petraș

His entire cultural and poetic journey places him in that category of poets who are unique and identifiable through their remarkable creations. Dan Marius Drăgan

Ion Cristofor is one of the most valuable poets hailing from the prestigious Echinox group of the 1980s. [...] He is, however, a poet of late modernity, a mannerist and an aesthete. [...] The poet is no stranger to postmodern techniques, but they are incorporated into metaphorical discourse, sumptuous and imaginative, solemn and grave. [...] Irony, when it is used, has a Romantic essence, it never relaxes into parody or gratuitous lucidity. Petru Poantă

Cristofor's poetry is a mixture of metaphorical lyricism and postmodern irony which seeks to desecrate. Adina Dinițoiu

Ion Cristofor's first stylistic quality is originality. It is comprised of the transposition of traditional values in an urban realm and in a dying world. As in Indian mythology, this universe heads towards the end of a cycle of time, kaliyuga. In the poet's vision, we are situated in the age of iron - the very last. Lucian Gruia

Also by Ion Cristofor

Poetry

O picătură de sânge/una gota de sangre. Grinta Publishing House, 2019. Romania. Bilingual edition [Spanish].

Am rand der kaffeetasse, Dionysus Publishing House, 2018. Germany, bilingual edition [German].

Gramofonul de pământ. Editura Limes Publishing House, 2014. Romania.

Sărbătoare la ospiciu. Casa Cărţii de Ştiinţă Publishing House, 2004. Romania.

Cronica stelelor, Editura Şcoala Ardeleană Publishing House, 2017. Romania.

Nopţi de jazz, Grinta Publishing House, 2015. Romania, bilingual edition [French].

Viaţa de rezervă, Editura Napoca Star, 2018.

Somewhere a blind child

Selected poems by Ion Cristofor

Translated by Andreea Iulia Scridon

Naked Eye Publishing

© Ion Cristofor 2021
Translation © Andreea Iulia Scridon 2021

All rights reserved

Book design and typesetting by Naked Eye

Cover illustration: painting by Maria Pal

ISBN: 9781910981146

www.nakedeyepublishing.co.uk

Acknowledgements

Some of these poems have previously been published in:

O picătură de sânge/una gota de sangre. Grinta Publishing House, 2019. Romania. Bilingual edition [Spanish].

Am rand der kaffeetasse, Dionysus Publishing House, 2018. Germany, bilingual edition [German].

Gramofonul de pământ. Editura Limes Publishing House, 2014. Romania.

Sărbătoare la ospiciu. Casa Cărții de Știință Publishing House, 2004. Romania.

Cronica stelelor, Editura Școala Ardeleană Publishing House, 2017. Romania.

Nopți de jazz, Grinta Publishing House, 2015. Romania. Bilingual edition [French].

Viața de rezervă, Editura Napoca Star, 2018.

Poeme Canibale, 2021.

SOMEWHERE A BLIND CHILD

Contents

Translator's Note 17
Late 19
The mermaid 20
My beloved lady 21
Communism 22
It's obvious 23
Cain's advice for his son 24
The butterfly 25
I don't have time 26
In the black mouth 27
The cherry tree 28
All illusions 29
Exodus 30
The dogs' undertaker 31
A tree's guests 32
I look around 33
Our roads lead mysterious ways 34
Meeting the stoics 36
Pointless sciences 38
Desolation 39
We wanted 40
Always 41
The black angel 42
Benjamin Fondane 43
I'm not the man 44
Eternal night 45
Nocturnal sky 46
Conversing with the fish of the sea 47
Infinite tenderness 48
Smoking fields 49
Marooned on Lampedusa 50
The most faithful wife 51
Cello suite 52
Somewhere a blind child 53
Your scent 54

Late (II)	55
The blind	56
The scribe's testament	57
Steam train	58
Vintage postcard	59
The wind is blowing	60
Your shadow	61
The last book	62

Translator's Note

Translating this selection of Ion Cristofor's poems revealed to me an accomplished and serious poet who, while being certain of his own convictions, leaves the door open to possibility; to the nuances and the surprise encounters in lived life. Through his simultaneous operation on multiple earthly and heavenly planes, Cristofor gives his reader the opportunity to penetrate the porous texture of his vision again and again, for there is always more beneath the surface of each of these poems.

Critic Niculina Oprea observes that the serious-minded Cristofor lives 'conscientiously', and that he benefits from an impressive imagistic palette, while Petru Poantă notes the complex, reflexive structure of his poems, created 'obsessively' as though in an imaginary laboratory, the key to his practice being that he 'discovers the world as he discovers the poem'. Multiple commentators note Cristofor's duality: sarcasm meets lyricism; melancholy meets optimism; metaphor meets plain-spokenness; old meets new. Mircea Diaconu identifies an 'archaic substratum' underlying Cristofor's poetic opus, permeated as it is with scriptural illusions. The ever-present sensuality and spirituality in Cristofor's recurrent natural world is the reason for him being termed a 'modern Christian poet'. It is his poetry's curious mix of cynicism and utopianism (and his compassion, stemming from the latter) that both qualifies him as a member of, and sets him apart from, Romania's leading 'Eighties Generation' of confessional poets who endured the harshest part of the communist regime and witnessed and wrote about the events preceding and following the 1989 Revolution.

In fact, 'Christian humanist' might more accurately describe Cristofor, who has never been afraid to take up a cause. Critic Roni Căciulari praises Cristofor's 'profound involvement in his immediate world', with Nicolae Manolescu describing Cristofor's poetic response to his country's communist legacy as 'sophisticated and informed'. A self-assured seeker who, steadfast and determined, has built his work upon the foundations of his most authentic self, Ion Cristofor is a poet to be welcomed with open arms into the Anglophone world.

In this translation I have endeavoured to stay as faithful as possible to the original texts while transmuting idiomatic meaning as I was best able. As this is a collection of selected poems, punctuation style varies from poem to poem since they are drawn from different collections and moments in the author's artistic life. Rather than homogenising them, I have chosen to transcribe each as it appears in the original in order to reflect developments that took place over time.

Andreea Iulia Scridon

20th December, 2020

Late

it's too late for me to descend from the cross
it's too early for me to rise again

my forehead shines in the shadow
like the leathery skin of a dog
like the rock polished by sacrifices
like the shaved wood of a coffin

I sit with a gun to my head
a poppy between my lips
with fingers of ash and I write and I write

and suddenly, night descends
and suddenly, emptiness descends
it's far too late my love
for us to rise again.

The mermaid

When I arrived home I found, to my surprise,
a mermaid asleep in my bed.
I called my manservant and screamed with indignation
Since when do you bring women here in my absence?

Calm yourself, Sir, he told me, it is simply an illusion.
One of your metaphors, misleading like all metaphors.
We headed to the bedroom and, to my consternation,
the enchanting mermaid had gone.
Only the blue duvet on my bed retained the traces
of her body, half-woman, half-fish.

I instantly gave my insolent servant the sack.

But sometimes at night the sound of waves tumbles into the
        bedroom
and a maddening mermaid's song keeps me awake.
Like Odysseus, I've come to stuff my ears with plugs.

It's either old age or nerve trouble,
said my friend, who is an accountant

My beloved lady

Someone pulls the night and its stars
over us like a quilt
Now the poem is but a hunting hawk
falling asleep
on my right hand
As my body is nothing but
a flesh-and-bones perch
on which the so young and seductive
and lovely lady clings,
my beloved lady
or the lady with the scythe.

Communism

I came home full of enthusiasm
my backpack crammed with red-covered brochures
from my Marxism-Leninism seminars.

For three hours
comrade teacher explained to us
with contagious pathos
that God doesn't exist
that nobody up to now has seen him
that not even the great Soviet cosmonauts
have seen him anywhere in cosmic space.

Once home I communicated the news
full of enthusiasm to my grandfather
who was praying, in a retrograde way,
on the tattered hassock in the corner.
I yelled at him plain and simple
comrade teacher told us that
God doesn't exist.

He continued to pray unperturbed
asking me when he finished
with a benign smile
whether eggs in the store exist,
whether meat at the butcher's exists,
or butter...

It's obvious

it's obvious that poetry won't open a bank account for you
it's obvious that poetry is nothing more than an old whore
it's obvious that Mrs Justice visits the casino frequently
it's obvious that the way has been paved for all catastrophes

it's obvious that priests don't bless the humble dandelion
it's obvious that sharks dominate the ocean
it's obvious that truth is a good that has no value
it's obvious that God gets no erotic phonecalls

it's obvious you can't get shut of your ulcer your shitty verses
    and your flu
it's obvious you can't shut out all of your uncertainties
it's obvious the government works day and night for the public
    good
it's obvious you should keep your mouth shut

pay your taxes cross yourself with your comrades
wipe your nose wipe the mud off your boots
take your pills at night

it's obvious the government will lead us all
to the gate of the cemetery called Eternity

Cain's advice for his son

May you always keep with you your swords and your ploughshares,
the knife and the whip, the bread and salt
but especially the gravestone
take it wherever you go
over land and sea
especially for the toil of the spring season
plowing harrowing seeding
when you disturb with your iron plough
the peace of those hidden beneath the furrow

And above all do not forget when you are tired at noon
to sleep with your head on the stone that bears your name
letting the wind rummage through your hair
letting it shift restlessly down the lines of your palms
letting it spit on you to ward off spells
in love with you
son of Cain

while death will plough furrows
cursing defiant bulls with dirty words
lashing a whip at the swords
coaxing ploughshares along with honeyed words
it will harrow it will sow it will weed

then at the sun's decline
death will yell from the other end of the pasture
you sloth the grain has ripened
enter the field with your scythe
as you would the woman you're dreaming of

The butterfly

Your lips
on the edge of the coffee cup
fluttered like a red butterfly.

It was then that I uttered for you
every word for love in the dictionary
and none of them became man.

After that, night fell,
my darling,
and the new moon rose above the city.

I don't have time

I don't have time to learn foreign tongues anymore,
I can accept that the only universal language is death's silence.

I don't feel like bowing to the graven images on TV anymore,
my gods are in a completely different place.

I don't have the patience to obey your harsh orders anymore.
In this life I was always unfaithful, even to the Lord's ten
        commandments.

I don't have the wealth or will to buy myself eternity anymore,
I can accept I'm growing older, along with the stones I tread on.

I don't have the strength to see Truth
spat in the face.
I spit in the faces of those who humiliate the truth.

In the black mouth

I stand in the tunnel's black mouth
and wait patiently for the night train to pass.

All those who translate from dead languages
are currently crowding my house's staircase.

Attention gentlemen
I yell to the mechanics asleep in the locomotive:
the poet is fragile as paper
in the teeth of flames.
The poet is hard as a diamond
in the mouth of tyrants.

The cherry tree

A tobacco field was rustling behind us.
Now, a troop of raucous soldiers
is climbing the hill shrouded in fog.
Under the blooming cherry tree in the yard
the old man was playing music on the gramophone.
Now, the sun on the metal rooftop
is turning like a record
beneath the patter of homing pigeons.
I will never know who it is I love
now, when the wind is going bezerk,
rumpling newspapers,
dancing on metal rooftops,
shamelessly lifting women's skirts.
Yet I'm heading towards you,
my palms open like a child,
with the promise of blossom which,
blown from a branch,
sails down towards the mud
but leaves behind the promise of fruit.

All illusions

I have seen butterflies tremble
over dead bodies
I have seen cigarettes smoulder
still lit
in the mouths of the hanged
I have seen the Venus de Milo
at work in a whorehouse
and the smouldering heads of humans
I have seen the sun rise
at midnight
like a wick in a candle
all illusions burned down
all words.

Exodus

what secret exodus is brewing
I asked you and the moon rose
enormous like a boat with sails
from among forests among rocks and houses

on a long and slender thread
like a giant spider
like an enormous red crab
from among hills among trees
and rocks the moon rose

and its atrocious, unearthly light
separating waves of water from each other
through a complex algorithmic programme
whose secret code
I couldn't crack for the life of me

I was waiting for mama to wake me up
in her child's body
when, suddenly aged, she whispered to me
my son
as if through a spyglass

as if through an enormous blue lens
time like a tide rolls within us.

for a moment I discerned in her teardrop
scenes ranging through The Last Supper
to the terrors of Judgment Day.

The dogs' undertaker

A coffin shop on the town's fringe –
inside, the bored manager flips playing cards,
he reads his own palm and yells
incomprehensible words in a semitic language
from time to time like a madman

Come ye master of dogs to the celestial slum
(it sounds like a poem by mihai ursachi the pelican)
to my tired lamp and bark
sadnesses dust melancholy avoiding our eyes

In the evening when the shadows of the dead flow downstream
like the long barges carrying grains piles of shiny coal
the unseen river on which trees and corpses flow together
come ye master of dogs I yell
sit on your haunches and bark in the shadowy corner of some shadowy phrase
or get the hell out of here and into the heart of terror
beyond the ocean's reach

Mihai Ursachi was a famous Romanian poet of Ion Cristofor's generation.

A tree's guests

her healing gods hadn't been born yet
that spring
we were a tree's guests

every night the beautiful stranger would embrace you
her heart was a pigeon coop

oh, her whispers that transported me to cloud nine
and the buds of her breasts that caught fire
in my palms

the black butterfly scattered these things at daybreak
with its zigzagged flight
writing in the light that had just opened its eyes
the strange hieroglyphs of death

in the mornings when the beautiful stranger would abandon me
on the kitchen table
grains of rice

glistened like pearls
to this day I still think they were real pearls

her healing gods hadn't been born yet
that spring when we were a tree's happy guests

I look around

I look around in wonder, God,
How perfect it all is
Radiating with beauty around my imperfection
What a jeweller's work the ant
That has just climbed, unperturbed, up the tip of my boot
How perfect all these blades of grass are
Letting themselves be crushed without protesting.

It's only me, God, whom you've given two eyes full of sadness
With which I admire the wonders you've created
And these flames which dance before me
With the sheen of golden ingots
With the violence of regrets.

Our roads lead mysterious ways

oh Lord there was a time when I too
bowed before the glitter of her whore's fingernails
our roads led us mysterious ways like those of the night butterfly

now the pearl merchant is exhausted
the remains of the rose are exhausted in the hand of the man
holding the cleaver

in the wind the soul bathes in doubt it bends over
and the birds haven't yet invented the sky

the morning bells dig mole tunnels in the clouds
your soul is clean like the lamb in its pen
like the sprig of basil in the old peasant woman's hand
taken full of dew to morning mass

believe and venture
you bend like a reed in the wind seeking
the faces of the stars it's grown dark near your house now
unrest breathes through the pores of our syllables
the sludge and the stones cry with an unbearably human voice
the willow laments with an old hag's voice

morning rises again evening falls again once we were young
I remember as if in another life I was a tree that bent in a storm

from my window in the evening I look out at the solemn faces of
          idiocy
brutality satisfies its every whim in its impeccable tuxedo
scoundrels grin in the limousine their consciences are up for
          bidding
now the beast brings its victim roses

while you Lord have screwed the moon in like a lightbulb
you've swept the stars up and let the birds of prey out

our roads go mysterious ways like those of the night butterfly.

Meeting the stoics

I'd like to leave for a remote island, but now isn't the right
    moment.
I've got nothing going for me anymore. I drink too much and
    read the Stoics.
My wife has left me and thieved all my books.
She's had enough of my free-loading ways. She melted away
    all the money I made.
You'll die of hunger with your poetry, she'd scream.
I realise she was right, poor woman.
She left for Spain to earn some dosh.

Now I'm free to go, but it isn't the right moment.
I drink too much and read Stoic philosophy.
I wonder what those guys meant when they wrote
"Live in harmony with nature".

Maybe I should have lived in harmony with my wife's
    histrionics.
But I'm not Zenon from Kition and I sure don't have the virtues
    of a Stoic.
Instead of a wife, Plato possessed three slaves.

I'd gladly leave everything and go
like Iambulus to the Islands of the Sun.
Iambulus was a Hellenised Arab merchant,
very rich, it seems.
Damn, I say to myself, these Arabs always know what to do

with philosophy, with business and with women.
The time this guy lived in was Eden on earth.
In the language of these Heliopolitans you could hear sounds
    birds would make.
They never married, they lived happily, in bountiful equality.
As a former communist, I almost envy these wise Solarians.

But we, we who lived in a world in which some were more
        equal than others.
Poor us.
I pity myself. I drink too much, make far too little money.
I'd slit my veins open like the wise Stoic Seneca.
Maybe I need a disciple like Nero's, who'd order me to do it.

With these guys now, not even suicide is what it used to be.
I realize that not even the Stoics make sense anymore.
Today they'd die of hunger, with all their philosophy.
In fact even our president
has recently criticised the unfortunate excess of philosophers.

These are utopias which one day I will have to throw out
the window.

Pointless sciences

you will die alone like a fly trapped in the double glazing
a fly that's buzzing desperately this afternoon

at the hour in which the wise Heraclitus of Ephesus discovers
that everything passes, everything flows
that you can't bathe twice in the same river

what river is this in which we're bathing
what river flows noisily through our lives

an otter is quietly breathing in your veins
your nerves are a basketful of eels
your silence shelters a cloister of celibate pelicans

what river is this which washes from our feet
the dour judges of a pointless science
what river kidnaps our lovers and takes them to Hades
what ruinous flood, what stream
murky with desires and dread
spurs us on from behind whining

rebellious students who have gone blind with their books in their
    arms,
crushed by volumes with gold-embossed spines
with bookmarks that don't teach us
how to pass away gracefully
with the eternal gentility
of dying roses

Desolation

the cloud was a brother to me the whole afternoon
then God beat it to who knows where
decked with gold and with teardrops

hungover, I listened to the sea's distant breath
my ear honed to the cries of the shipwrecked

beyond the stone window
the pale stars were swallowing the great desolation
that was on its way over to join the night inside you
like an army of Hoplites like a terrible horde
like an unseen Macedonian phalanx

when suddenly sleep snatched me up in haste
with a dark hand it pulled me down into the vortex

just as the season was hurling its last coins
into the open palm of Judas

we wanted

we wanted to bring the sky down between us
there where minor gods chattered on the doorstep
accompanied by blind moles and flutes

but the hands no longer recognised the fingers
the son no longer recognised his mother blinded by her love for him
the bow recognised neither its arrow nor its wound

as the days waned barbarous exhortations resounded
and bloody songs of insurrection

and at night we danced drunk on the tightrope between two worlds
blindly we followed the screams and gasps of the deaf

but the sundays oh the sundays inhabited by wails
then we listened to the birds sing madly
on altars abandoned by gods and men

Always

The passage of hours yawns a solitude within us
like the yawn of a wildcat
or like the ground when an earthquake hits

Always the same hours scattered with decomposing leaves
by skulls lined up by betrayals and crimes

And the brass band of now blunted senses
playing to exhaustion
in a pub full of smoke of boredom of disgust

A pub on the outskirts of the century
in which Ivan murders his neighbour Jochan in cold blood
in which Jochan murders Itzik in cold blood
in which the warm blood of an erratic history flows through us all

And a merciful unknown God returns
an old and bearded man from Siberia
hesitating before the empty noose of the gallows
the booby trap in the bush which cries
delirious in a foreign language
under the bitter wind's merciless whip

And the blue or hunted soul
oh our poor soul like the country mouse
or the rabbit terrified before the gun
our soul screams to the empty moon
with a pack of famished wolves

The black angel

Like the petals of a wild rose, old wounds, regrets, open
in your wide open eye – the great nothingness,
the heartless bloody harrier
hovers over the prey.

While a wandering group of wise men of troubadours
plucked from seedy pubs
come together out of the road's dust
a heavenly light announces itself to you.

In the train station of Chitila village
the black angel makes a pit-stop
smokes a cigarette in boredom and leaves.

Get the hell out of here he whispers to me in passing
leave this dreary place.

Your pain has no sisters no brothers
nor a garden of olives from which to hang the noose for your
neck.

Benjamin Fondane

Like the butterflies rushing through the spring light
you leave me, useless words
heading for the clouds that glow like a knife's blade

And you, Barbu Fundoianu, smile childishly at death
on a train platform in Paris
you wave at us
we who have already arrived in the last stop of hell.

From the railcar's ladder
I implore you, brothers of mine,
pinched peddlers of miracles,
open the door to an old poet –
his mouldy moth-eaten coat
protects the stars and the earth.

His wounds from Salamis
the scar inherited from the ghetto's cellars
the ashes of his body burned at Auschwitz, at Hiroshima

behold the glittering medals which
the Swedish Academy of the clouds
award you on your doorstep without trumpets or fanfare.

I'm not the man

I'm not the man who drowns in the ocean of a teardrop
I'm not the man who hangs himself in the cow shed
I'm not the man lighting a candle now.

holy mother of terrors
I'm not the man who gets shipwrecked on a dark night
and no way am I the man who cannot return

to the body of the man who wrote these words
that tremble like a butterfly on the face of a sleeping soldier.

Eternal night

As if on command
A further dog emerged from the barking dog.
A further bird flew out of the bird.
From black earth, black earth is born.

That's what happens some nights here.
From a railway carriage dragging along a disused line
emerges the unicorn, immaculate as milk,
being barely restrained by a naked woman,
her long hair, her golden hair sweeping the train tracks
that glint beneath the moon like a razor
on a man's shadowy face.

That's what happens sometimes in these empty places
when the magical song of crickets in the heathland
triggers the pistons of the steam engines
and suddenly the travellers
friends and our long-dead relatives
wave farewell from the carriage's lit windows.
They flutter handkerchiefs – for a few moments only
then the train, with a long whistle,
re-enters the empire, starlit with stars,
of the eternal night.

Nocturnal sky

The moon's sickle
passes impassively over the grain field.

The quail chicks are terrified
by Sputnik's passage
over the sky.

Conversing with the fish of the sea

Gently, almost indiscernibly, phosphorus blinks within our bones
conversing with the fish of the sea, with violet stars
in the darkness that draws a fine fishing net
over our wounds.
Autumn sends – cascading down the marble steps –
rotten fruit, a mummified child, a king's skull
as someone drums all night long in despair
someone crawls on their hands and knees.
It's time to switch the lamp off and go to sleep
the bones of the temples, bickering amongst themselves,
have begun to think like evergreens
like swallows ready to leave for warm countries.

Like a procession of candles in snow
like a row of crania
in the catacombs is the book, full of letters and lines,
on which you rest your weary head, as on a sarcophagus.

Infinite tenderness

Cheerful is the demon who whispers
drink, drink, drink all the darkness inside you
then pick up the trumpet and play
perched on the wall of a leper colony
until your tongue and your lips bleed.

Return at last to that house
of worry, of dark melancholy
and rest your tired head on the tabletop
let it whiten on the mound of rustling wisdom
listening to the teardrop as it falls along with the eyeball
on stones dulled by bones in prayer.

Listen as the distant emptiness draws closer
with a woman's steps, with feline steps
listen as the dead psalmodise in the abyss.

The darkness takes your hand with infinite tenderness,
as if you were its own cosseted child.

Smoking fields

Autumn fields smoulder on the horizon
under a sorely bruised moon
as if after a lost battle

swine flu has infiltrated the palace's upper stories
the newspapers and televisions are coughing somewhere
castrated voices echo in the sombre corridors

every word is now a storm of shouting
a scream splitting open the sac near a shimmering body of water

the tree in the courtyard discovers its funereal brass and wind
        instruments

dry branches slam into the void of your disbelief
and your skin sings wildly and obliviously
as if it were the central being in a celestial light
near the campfire of some lonely shepherds

singing as if given an unexpected home among the cobbles
among the leaves drifting aimlessly down the streets
among housewives lounging like sows in the ever more
        confining gloom.

Marooned on Lampedusa

The Evening News has made you happy.
You breathe a sigh of relief that your name
is not listed among the dead.
The wind will stop blowing
tomorrow, the smiling broadcaster assures us.
Her breasts seem to confirm the news.

The earthquake has avoided us once more
Japan is quaking in its bones.

I see the hands of my friends in Kyoto trembling at their writing
          desks.
Here, the government's earthquake is imminent.

Until then, see the washed-up corpses being recorded in
          Lampedusa,
lined up on the quays like vegetables in green plastic sacks.

I wonder what I should ask the good Lord for after all this
since it's time for my prayers.
This evening the stars have aligned in my window
governed by a formula whose equation is a mystery to me.

As it is, death has harassed other people all day
God, I don't know what to ask you for this evening, maybe a
          woman
but the Bible says it's a sin and I don't understand why.
It must be a transcription error by monks in the Middle Ages.
I give up on praying, take my pills, turn the lamp off,
thinking of the woman expelled from my monotonous life
by those fussy monks with their crotchety goose quills,
from my spacious bed
in which sleep embraces me like a green plastic sack…

The most faithful wife

She follows me with a dog's fidelity
she, the only woman in my life
who puts up with all my flaws.

Not once did I heard her complain
that I didn't buy her the right jewel
that I didn't serve her coffee in bed.

I don't remember her ever reproaching me
for not bringing her flowers on her birthday.

She looks into my eyes with a love
I never found in any other woman.

When I came home drunk
she never scolded me, never cast me off
she followed me like a loyal shadow
from my early youth on.

A few days ago she left me speechless with awe
when out of nowhere
my darling
awarded me The Legion of Honour.

She is without a shadow of a doubt the best wife
and possibly the most loyal lover I've ever had.

Her name
is Poverty.

Cello suite

The cello caught fire
in the tree at the entrance to the orchard the birds
suddenly fell silent.

Lord, the pebbles before my house
have fallen in love with a girl.

The walls light up when she opens the door to me
the books on the shelves begin to dance
and the livid flowers in the vase have started to float through the air.

When she undresses on the couch
the blossom-laden trees all move into my bedroom
their love-sick leaves becoming delirious.

It's autumn, Lord, it's so late in heaven
and love is a blue orange in your hand,
a poem without lines.

The cello caught fire
in the tree before the orchard
the birds suddenly went silent.

Somewhere a blind child

In these days, the season with its hoary hands
reads to us in a whisper the names written in the book of the
　　　　dead
a lonely heart is howling like a dog.

Somewhere a blind child
is spelling out his name in a school catalogue
Homer
in Arabic script…

A generous young woman
her breasts like two mounds of salt licked at by goats
is smilingly offering,
for almost nothing, a passport to heaven.

A moaning and a stabbing pain are giving us a haven in our
　　　　home village
a sunny place a verdant place
a cart pulled by two women and a horse
an iron seat below the guillotine ahead.

But we wait feverish
at the post office for a parcel containing Tutankhamun's mummy
a band of gypsies sings in the withered orchard
a flock of starlings brings the final decree the final rumour.

But look now it's growing late in the books that I never ended up
　　　　writing
the sun rises on the continent that I never found
all the women I never loved left me.

In these days, the wise men and the blind prophets
crawl into the sun that has now set
stars rise in my sadness
all the women I once loved have left me.

Your scent

A child walks
cup of milk in hand
through the scent of your body.

Only now have I understood the ancients
who wrote that divinity
is simply an image of beauty.

Late (II)

Your cheek is but a semi-precious stone
weathered by insomnia

phantom voices waft through deserted gardens
or perhaps the day's guards force truth into the night's cell

the last calligraphies of the empire are crumpled in your closet
the last emperor hallucinates in your moth-eaten clothes

in the evening a pope plays with shoals of fish
in the marble basin of a silvery bay

the moon is now rising on the rue gauguin
the caws of the jackals telling how very late it is.

The blind

All night I heard the blind wandering down the corridors
smacking their canes against walls and windows,
the throne was abandoned in the pantry,
everything resounded emptily,
it seemed nobody was home.

For the hosts had left with the young thieves
starting out before the sun
with their defiant little lanterns.

All night and all day the blind stumble bewildered
into corners into drawers into closets and murmur
where is the purple where is the golden yarn,
what to do,
we wondered, with the pontifical bastards.

We bowed before the prayer rug,
we flattered death with honeyed words,
we coaxed her with a few dry pretzels,
with a few bloodied flags.

Oh, what a sinister story, what bothersome spectres
my bedstead is creaking.
We will have to move in the night
to other rooms to other countries to other life-stories.

The scribe's testament

To Liliane Wouters

All of my books burned
in the Great Library in Alexandria
from the very first to the very last.

All that has remained of me is ash
and the dust which – look – now speaks to you
in all the languages on earth, on every road
stronger than kings or Persian armies
the dust that enters your mouth, your eyes, blinding you.

And – look – I the great scribe have come
to fritter time away, a barking dog in Alexandria now.
I've become the companion of corpse-washers
of grave-robbers, of foul-mouthed whores
I, who laid the stones for the glory of the pharaohs
have become a lousy good-for-nothing, the scribe out to grass.

I leave this dark story to my son
myopic love child by the name of Homer
I leave to him this raft of ashes
my harem of mermaids and the sea
and the window of the hut wide open to the sky.

Steam train

Sometimes at night
a strange steam train
passes black as hell
in front of my fog-drowned house.

From a train window,
Rimbaud waves to me desperately
I'll be waiting for you in Al Habash he cries
with a fresh shipment of guns.

Another time from the open window
Lord Byron's wavy hair makes an appearance
he tells me that soon
there will be a terrible battle in Missolonghi
he asks if I'm ready to die
but there's no time for me to answer him.

A few nights ago
from the window of the last carriage
with a map in his hand
I saw for a moment
the enlightened Rasputin of geographies
Robert Goffin
grown more and more disgusted by whiny poets
he didn't even glance at me.

It seems almost yesterday
that the face of a Greek man grown old before his time
Konstantinos P. Kavafis
disappeared in the moon-illumined night
assuring me
with a complicit smile
that preparing for the barbarians is pointless
they are already among us.

Vintage postcard

A piano
flung onto to the riverbank
by a few labourers

the new occupants of the house
surrendered by a bourgeois family
who were taken to the Gulag.

And the waterfall
mourning night-long
on rhythms of Bach.

The wind is blowing

To the poet Ayten Mutlu

The wind is blowing over the province's dark plains.
Alone, utterly mute,
the scribe spits in his own inkwell.
Doubt has crept in between the psalms,
a white phantom passes through the rooms
reminding you of an hour of love
that once passed over you like a galloping herd of horses,
like a reckless ocean wave.
And now flocks of starlings proclaim you governor of the
          province
and towards evening the clouds send you dark ambassadors.
With its child's hands the gentle rain seeks out the crown of your
          head
white before your time.
An empire falls at the feet of a woman dressed in black.

Your shadow

I sit in your shadow
like a violin sits in its black box.

The old apple tree has flowered,
people have turned into birds
overnight.

A gap in the clouds
allows the moon to penetrate the poet's room
and read him the end of the poem.

The last book

It seems the heavenly ark is shuddering
in its very bones.

The wind rustles in every nook, like the Secret Police of old
who read our last book beside the hearth
in which logs burn, or are they human heads?

A woman with violet hair, with freshly done nails
asks after you at the prison door.

The carnival day masks have been labelled and filed
in the small provincial museum
bearing the name of an unknown artist.

On the commuter train
amidst peasant women with baskets of chickens and turkeys
Arthur Rimbaud has just arrived

And I suddenly wonder why
every time
I dial the good Lord's phone number
the same woman's voice picks up.

I think of the gypsies that passed through our village in my
    childhood,
the young gypsy girls wearing cowry shells.
In front of the rusty mirror I wonder
if it wasn't them after all who stole my child's face.

In the scaffolds of a ruined temple
a few bats look for a resting place.
And poets' souls rise so lightly into the sky,
like coloured balloons let go by a child.

You, my hypocritical brothers, brace yourselves and offer a piece
       of your bread
to the rich.
This evening my heart is breaking for those who are poor
in spirit
for only they write the most passionate love letters
and only they have the most beautiful, devoted wives
waiting for them at home.

In this godforsaken town ignored by the world of money,
preparations are made for the last supper
beneath a sky galvanised by storms.

A choir of wise men sings dirty songs
in the garret of an esteemed professor,
drunk from so much metaphysics.

And again I wonder if the dead,
those who all their lives hated each other ferociously
at least shake hands in forgiveness, in the eleventh hour,
beneath the earth.

Naked Eye Publishing
A fresh approach

Naked Eye Publishing is an independent not-for-profit micro-press intent on publishing quality poetry and literature, including in translation. We are also developing a 'Potted Theses' series: academic theses rewritten for the general reader.

A particular focus is translation. We aim to take a midwife role in facilitating the translation of works that have until now been disregarded by English-language publishing. We will be happy if we function purely as an initial stepping-stone both for overlooked writers and first-time literary translators.

Each of us at Naked Eye is a volunteer, competent and professional in our work practice, and not intending to make a profit for the press. We see ourselves as part of the revolution in book publishing, embodying the newly levelled playing field, sidestepping the publishing establishment to produce beautiful books at an affordable price with writers gaining maximum benefit from sales.

nakedeyepublishing.co.uk

www.ingramcontent.com/pod-product-compliance
Lightning Source LLC
Chambersburg PA
CBHW071756080526
44588CB00013B/2266